The Learnertainment® Pocket Tip Book

101 Tips to Make Learning Engaging & Effective

By Lenn Millbower,
the Learnertainment® Trainer

www.OffbeatTraining.com

Copyright © Lenn Millbower

All rights reserved. No part of this book may be reprinted or reproduced in any form or by any electronic, mechanical, or other means, now known or hereafter invented, including photocopying, recording, and information storage and retrieval, without written permission in writing from the publisher.

ISBN 978-0-557-44582-7

Offbeat Training LLC
3329 Oakpoint Circle
Davenport, Florida 33837-8690

Offbeat Training® is a registered trademark of Offbeat Training LLC

About The Author

Lenn Millbower

From Disney training leader to published author, from musician-magician to college professor, Lenn Millbower's lauded Learnertainment® techniques have taught business leaders, trainers, educators and presenters how to keep their audience awake so their message can take.

Lenn's published works include *ASTD InfoLine: Music as a Training Tool*, *The CLOUT Competencies Inventory©*, *Cartoons for Trainers*, *Game Show Themes for Trainers*, *Show Biz Training*, and *Training with a Beat*.

Lenn is a popular professional speaker, with successful presentations at many international conferences and for clients worldwide.

Lenn is a creative learning leader formerly with Disney World, an accomplished music arranger-composer, a professional entertainer, and the president of Offbeat Training LLC.

Offbeat Training LLC
329 Oakpoint Circle
Davenport, FL 33837
www.OffbeatTraining.com
Lenn@OffbeatTraining.com

Index

The Learnertainment® Eight

Listed below are the eight principles of Learnertainment®, their associated action steps, and the page where the tips for each action step begin.

Emotion Creates Memory:
Evoke Emotion .... Page 1

Perspectives Deepen Meaning:
Layer Learning .... Page 9

Visuals Aid Retention:
Present In Pictures .... Page 19

Suggestions Guide Outcomes:
Make It Magical .... Page 37

The Environment Talks:
Stage The Surroundings .... Page 45

Sound Trumps Sight:
Mix In Music .... Page 51

Laughter Produces Positivity:
Harness Humor .... Page 65

Professionalism Produces Results:
Perfect Your Performance ...... Page 83

Learnertainment® Explained

That's Learnertainment®

Learnertainment®, the fusion of learning and entertainment, is based on the principles I developed as an entertainer, performing throughout the United States. As a nightclub act, our pacing had to be fast and furious.

Years later, as a Disney training leader and a college professor, I realized that there wasn't much difference between nightclub goers and learners: both have short attention spans.

I began applying the principles of entertainment to learning and my success rates increased.

This tip book shares those successful entertainment techniques. May they help you *'Break a leg!'*

Dedication

This work is dedicated my father Leonard
who, among many other life lessons,
taught me a love for music.

Thank's Dad!

The Learnertainment Pocket Tip Book

Principle: Emotion Creates Memory

Action Step: Evoke Emotion

Emotion Creates Memory

Learnertainment® Tip 1:

If learners have a positive, emotional experience, the learning is more likely to be remembered.

When something emotional happens, the brain snaps to attention. It then compares what just happened to what it has experienced in the past. Once a comparison is made, the brain evaluates the experience for relevance and importance. If the event is worth remembering, it passes from short-term to long-term memory.

Where many experiences create negative emotion, entertainment is uniquely designed to create positive emotion. Learnertain™ them and you will create positive emotional experiences. Your content will then be more likely to be remembered.

Evoke Emotion

learnertainment® Tip 2:

Move your learners from panic to pleasure.

The human brain focuses on survival first, pleasure second. When entering a new environment for the first time, learners can be engulfed in fear, hesitancy, and negativity. The brain interprets these emotions as danger and it panics. Learning is extremely difficult when the brain is in this panic mode.

Make your learning environment welcoming, comforting, and enjoyable. This will move the brain from panic to pleasure. The result will be relaxed brains fully able to focus on learning.

Emotion Creates Memory

learnertainment® Tip 3:

Baby-sit the brain's negative tendencies so that learning can occur.

The brains neo-cortex includes a left and a right hemisphere. Generally speaking, the left hemisphere processes positive emotions like laughter and joy. The right processes negative emotions like fear and disgust. If the left perceives positive potential, adrenaline is released. If the right perceives negative potential, cortisol is released. Both chemicals sear memories into the brain.

Fortunately, the right hemisphere is also drawn to entertaining activities like cartoons, music, games, and mnemonics. Use them to keep the right hemisphere engaged. The left hemisphere can then focus without distraction on learning.

Evoke Emotion

learnertainment® Tip 4:

Provide emotional connections that align with what the learners really care about.

A movie works on two levels: *'what happens'* and *'what it means.'* *'What happens'* defines what the movie is about (i.e. a western in space; a beast must win true love). *'What it means'* delivers a deeper, holistic message (i.e. may the force be with you; beauty comes from within). The holistic message turns a move into a hit.

In learning, the objectives are *'what happens.'* The holistic *'what it means'* message is often missing. Align your learning program with a holistic need that will matter to your learners (i.e. live well; build better relationships). Your program will then be relevant to the organization AND your learners.

Lenn@OffbeatTraining.com

Emotion Creates Memory

learnertainment® Tip 5:

Use three-act movie structure to tell your learning story.

Movies tell their stories in four quadrants; *Prologue, Act One, Act Two*, and *Act Three*. The Prologue captures attention. *Act One* introduces the circumstances. *Act Two* puts the plot in motion. *Act Three* resolves the outstanding conflicts.

In a classroom, the *Prologue* captures attention. *Act One* teaches the concepts. *Act Two* provides hands on practice with the details. *Act Three* identifies specific applications the learners can apply to their lives.

Your role changes with each act as you move from motivator to expert, to coach, and finally, to cheerleader.

Evoke Emotion

learnertainment® Tip 6:

Avoid icebreakers. Don't break the ice; melt it.

Instead of selecting a generic icebreaker from a collection of activities, create a subject-focused introductory experience. Start with what the learners already know about the subject. Design an activity around that knowledge. The activity should peak learner curiosity and provide a holistic image of the subject to be taught. It should be interesting, exciting, and lead learners to conclude, *"I am curious about this and want to know more."* It should not teach details.

This process will avoid the pointless icebreakers learners resent. It will melt resistance and create a positive, eager-to-learn environment.

Lenn@OffbeatTraining.com

Emotion Creates Memory

learnertainment® Tip 7:

Give your learners time to connect what they learn to what they already know.

Your learners' brains—like all human brains—seek to relate what they are learning with what they already know. Each brain stores information in a way that makes sense to it. The new information is usually compared to older, already filed information. It is then placed in context with the old.

This sorting and filing takes time. When you pile detail upon detail, the time available for the brain to make and store these connections is compressed. The learners absorb less and less as their brains overload.

Keep your content at a minimum so that your learners get the connection time they need.

The Learnertainment® Pocket Tip Book

Principle: Perspectives Deepen Meaning

Action Step: Layer Learning

Perspectives Deepen Meaning

Learnertainment® Tip 8:

Use *Multiple Intelligences* to communicate in the way each learner prefers to learn.

Howard Gardner developed the theory of *Multiple Intelligences*. He stated that learners are smart in different ways; that learners who are engaged in the ways they are smart learn more effectively; and that learners should be exposed to all eight Intelligences.

Gardner labeled his Intelligences as *BODILY-KINESTHETIC*, *INTERPERSONAL*, *INTRAPERSONAL*, *LOGICAL-MATHEMATICAL*, *MUSICAL-RHYTHMIC*, *NATURALISTIC*, *VERBAL-LINGUISTIC*, AND *VISUAL-SPATIAL*.

Tips 9-16 provide suggestions for maximizing the individual intelligences in learning.

Layer Learning

learnertainment® Tip 9:

Use movement to appeal to learners with a high *BODILY-KINESTHETIC* intelligence.

Learners with a high *BODILY-KINESTHETIC* intelligence have difficulty staying still for long periods of time. They will be squirming in seat, drumming with pencils, and fiddling with table toys.

To engage these learners, use activities that involve hand-eye coordination, physical movement, and the handling of materials.

Lenn@OffbeatTraining.com

Perspectives Deepen Meaning

learnertainment® Tip 10:

Use interaction to appeal to learners with a high *INTERPERSONAL* intelligence.

Learners with a high *INTERPERSONAL* intelligence want to talk and share observations with other people. They will be observing the emotions of others, engaging in side conversations, and talking more than you wish they would.

To engage these learners, tell emotive stories, give them time to talk, and provide teamwork assignments.

Layer Learning

learnertainment® Tip 11:

Use reflection to appeal to learners with a high *INTRAPERSONAL* intelligence.

Learners with a high *INTRAPERSONAL* intelligence want to ponder and reflect on what they observe, feel, and think. They are the silent learners who—when they finally say something—surprise you with how much they have learned.

To engage these learners, provide time for self-assessment, personal reflection, and individual action planning.

Perspectives Deepen Meaning

learnertainment® Tip 12:

Use data to appeal to learners with a high *LOGICAL-MATHEMATICAL* intelligence.

Learners with a high *LOGICAL-MATHEMATICAL* intelligence respond best to factual information. They are the skeptics who want to know what the data suggests and search for logical conclusions.

To engage these learners, provide factual information, data to examine, and opportunities to reason problems through to a conclusion.

Layer Learning

learnertainment® Tip 13:

Use music to appeal to learners with a high *Musical-Rhythmic* intelligence.

Learners with a high MUSICAL-RHYTHMIC intelligence respond to harmonic tones, melodic phrases, and rhythmic patterns. They will be tapping their toes or humming while you present information.

To engage these learners, use rhymes, music cues, and rhythmic patterns of speech.

Read Tips 47-58—drawn from my book *Training With a Beat*—to discover musical applications that make learning more effective.

Perspectives Deepen Meaning

Learnertainment® Tip 14:

Use nature to appeal to learners with a high *NATURALISTIC* intelligence.

Learners with a high *NATURALISTIC* intelligence are extremely sensitive to the natural world around them. They will be gazing out the window, seeking connections to the natural world, and noticing the health of the plants—or lack of plants—in the room.

To engage these learners, use examples drawn from nature, display pictures of animals, and include ecological elements in your presentation.

Layer Learning

learnertainment® Tip 15:

Use language to appeal to learners with a high *VERBAL-LINGUISTIC* intelligence.

Learners with a high *VERBAL-LINGUISTIC* intelligence want to read, talk, and listen to others speak. They are voracious readers, attentive during lectures, and eager to talk when called upon.

To engage these learners, display quotes, use word puzzles, assign reading activities, and encourage discussion.

Perspectives Deepen Meaning

learnertainment® Tip 16:

Use visuals to appeal to learners with a high *VISUAL-SPATIAL* intelligence.

Learners with a high *VISUAL-SPATIAL* intelligence think in pictures and the alignment of visual elements. Crooked projection screens, poorly chosen visuals, and a cluttered room distract them.

To engage these learners, place attractive posters around the room, provide visual representations of models and content points, and use color appropriately. Tips 19-25 provide some guidelines for the application of color.

The Learnertainment® Pocket Tip Book

Principle: *Visuals Aid Retention*

Action Step: *Present In Pictures*

Visuals Aid Retention

learnertainment® Tip 17:

Communicate in visuals wherever possible.

Both words and pictures are visuals, but pictures communicate a message much more quickly. Words have to be decoded for meaning, translated into language, and then interpreted. A picture only needs to be decoded for meaning.

Substitute visuals for words wherever possible, but avoid visuals that are only remotely related to the content. Poorly chosen visuals may actually distract learners from your content point.

learnertainment® Tip 18:

Use color to communicate emotion.

People see color before content. Color communicates the emotion before words can be understood. People respond to color in two categories: light and warm for openness and comfort or dark and cool for aloofness and formality. Bright colors tend to spark energy and creativity while dark colors lower stress and increase feelings of peacefulness.

Tips 19-25 provide detailed information on the effective placement of color in learning situations.

Visuals Aid Retention

Learnertainment® Tip 19:

Use yellow to draw attention to key words, phrases, and visuals.

A learner's eyes are drawn to yellow before any other color. Use yellow to highlight important points, indicate key words the participants should write in their workbooks, and draw attention to visuals you want the learners to notice. Yellow also creates positive moods and encourages physical activity.

Yellow should not be overused. The resulting effect is like being shouted at visually. Be cautious also with yellow-blue combinations. The eyes have difficulty deciding which of the two colors to focus on.

Present In Pictures

learnertainment® Tip 20:

Use red for accents and highlights.

Red is an engaging and emotive color that commands attention. A hint of red on a presentation slide or poster suggests excitement. It draws the viewer in. Red also boosts creativity and spark bursts of short-term energy.

Red should not be overused. It has an aggressive quality to it that may generate unwanted anxiety. Be cautious with red-green and red-blue combinations. The eyes have difficulty deciding which of the two colors to focus on.

Lenn@OffbeatTraining.com

Learnertainment® Tip 21:

Use blue as a calming background color.

Blue communicates calm and a sense of well-being. It aids study, focusing concentration and encouraging deep thinking. A light font on a dark blue background provides a desirable mix of highly viewable and exciting text with a calming background.

Be careful not to overuse blue. It can be overly sedate. Be cautious with blue-red and blue-yellow combinations. The eyes have difficulty deciding which of the two colors to focus on.

Learnertainment® Tip 22:

Use green to help produce steady, long-term energy.

Green is a calming and reassuring color. It connotes the new growth and abundance of spring, the comfort of grass, and the rest and leisure of the summer. The subconscious implications of spring and growth make green an ideal color to enhance productivity and encourage steady, positive, long-term energy.

Be cautious with green-red combinations. The eyes have difficulty deciding which of the two colors to focus on.

Visuals Aid Retention

Learnertainment® Tip 23:

Use brown to communicate continuity.

Brown is a calming, comforting, color reminiscent of the earth. It connotes strength, solidity, and dependability.

Use brown to reaffirm continuity in situations where learners may be anxious about change or uncertainty.

learnertainment® Tip 24:

Use black to hide items or emphasize other colors.

Black is a dark, foreboding color, usually associated with villains. Black represents the absence of color. The eye often doesn't notice it. Use black to hide power cables, props, and other items you wish to draw attention away from.

Black is an excellent color to use in relief. It makes bright colors look brighter. When placed behind text and shapes, it provides dynamic shadows that make lighter images stand out.

Be careful when creating workbooks that will feature dark black text printed on bright white paper. The black-white combination can strain the eyes. Substitute a more subtle paper hue of light gray or crème.

Visuals Aid Retention

learnertainment® Tip 25:

Use white in handouts to create open space.

Where black represents villains and danger, white represents purity and cleanliness. Use white to create a sense of openness and air.

When combined with black, it is challenging for the eyes to look at. Rather than printing materials in dark black text on bright white paper, substitute a more subtle paper hue of light gray or crème.

Present In Pictures

learnertainment® Tip 26:

Use props to anchor knowledge.

Props are excellent visual and kinesthetic learning tools. Props capture attention, create vibrant metaphoric connections, provide physical manifestations of content, and, when used as tabletop toys, give kinesthetic learners something to dissipate their excess energy.

Use props to introduce subjects, make relevant points, and conclude learning segments.

Learning props should align with the *Offbeat Prop Selection Filter*™. Look for props that are *ORIGINAL*, *FUN*, *FOCUSED*, *BRAIN-BASED*, *EDUCATIONAL*, *ALIGNED* and *TANGIBLE*. Read Tips 27-33 to examine the *Offbeat Prop Selection Filter*™

Lenn@OffbeatTraining.com

Visuals Aid Retention

learnertainment® Tip 27:

Learning props should be *ORIGINAL*.

Any prop you select should be placed in a unique, original, and unconventional context. Strive for an unexpected application that peeks learner curiosity. When your learners first see the prop, they should be drawn towards it. They should want to know more about how that prop relates to the learning subject.

There are, of course, learning props that are exactly what they seem. When learners are being exposed to a cash register that they will use in their job, there is no point in camouflaging the usage. Those uses are expected and legitimate. But because they are expected, their enjoyment value is limited. For maximum value, seek out additional props your learners do not expect to see.

Present In Pictures

learnertainment® Tip 28:

Learning props should be *Fun*.

Any prop you select should evoke a feeling of positive emotion through fun. Fun props enhance learning, making it more playful and less threatening.

Props like bananas, glasses with an attached nose and mustache, hand buzzers, noisemakers, plungers, potatoes, hats, and oversized items are naturally fun. If there is a legitimate sway to use one of these items in your classroom, do so.

Visuals Aid Retention

learnertainment® Tip 29:

Learning props should be *FOCUSED*.

Any prop you select should support the learning point being made.

An interesting prop that does not align with the content will distract focus and disrupt learning.

Before you select a prop for inclusion in your learning program, verify that your reasons for using that prop are aligned with your content. You should also verify that your learners will comprehend the learning application when you explain it.

learnertainment® Tip 30:

Learning props should be *BRAIN-BASED*.

Any prop you select should deliver a logical and a holistic message. The prop should communicate factual information that illuminates the content. It should also provide a holistic visual of the learning point.

By carefully selecting a prop that works both logically and holistically, you will engage more brain cells and increase the possibility that your learning point will be remembered after the learning event has concluded.

Visuals Aid Retention

Learnertainment® Tip 31:

Learning props should be *EDUCATIONAL*.

Any prop you select should add information about the learning point being made. When you talk about an item, display it.

By displaying the item, you communicate more information than is possible with words alone. The result is a vibrant message successfully delivered.

learnertainment® Tip 32:

Learning props should be *ALIGNED*.

Any prop you select should match the mores of your learners. Norms are different throughout the world. They also vary from group to group. What will work for front line employees may not work for company executives.

Know your audience and select props that will align with your learners' societal, moral, and team norms. Otherwise, you risk offending your audience.

Visuals Aid Retention

learnertainment® Tip 33:

Learning props should be *TANGIBLE*.

Any prop you select should provide specific learning results. Even if a prop is carefully selected, it may not deliver the results you expect. Wherever possible, measure the effectiveness of your prop usage. Eliminate props that do not resonate with your learners.

Props are fun learning tools, but cannot be simply about fun. They must add value or you risk being perceived as frivolous by your learners.

The Learnertainment® Pocket Tip Book

Principle: *Suggestions Guide Outcomes*

Action Step: *Make It Magical*

Suggestions Guide Outcomes

Learnertainment® Tip 34:

Learner trust is your most important asset. Never violate it.

Magicians manipulate audiences. So do learning professionals. Where magicians '*trick*' audiences for enjoyment, trainers, teachers, and speakers manipulate learners to change behavior. Both audiences permit this manipulation as long as they perceive that the manipulation is for their benefit.

If you engage in a mindless activity, denigrate other participants, or display unprofessional behavior, you risk losing learner trust, and the ability to influence learning results.

Make It Magical

Learnertainment® Tip 35:

Make learning seem effortless.

Learning should occur as if by magic. Foster an open and welcoming environment. Avoid pointless activities. Address learner questions at the moment they are most likely to ask them. Keep the focus on learner skills and not your own superior abilities. Position the skills to be learned as reasonable and reachable.

Display absolute confidence in your learners' ability to master the subject matter. Celebrate learning achievements with excitement and as a confirmation of the learner's abilities. The result will be relaxed, confident, focused learners, and higher levels of satisfaction and learning retention.

Learnertainment® Tip 36:

Be completely congruent with your content.

A major factor in learning success is the instructor's alignment with the subject matter being taught. If you are hesitant about your knowledge of the subject, do not agree with some of the content points, or are bored with the presentation, your discomfort will be felt by the learners. This subconscious reaction is a distraction and will undercut what you are saying.

Be fully committed to—and passionate about—the content. If you aren't, how can you expect your learners to be?

Make It Magical

learnertainment® Tip 37:

Place your learners in charge of their own learning.

Create opportunities for your learners to be in control. Give them choices. Ask their opinions. Listen attentively and validate those opinions. Place them in teams, give them assignments, and get out of the way.

Talk less and structure learning so that the learners do more. The result will be higher learner satisfaction and more effective learning.

Suggestions Guide Outcomes

learnertainment® Tip 38:

Use magic to introduce content.

The *Change Bag* illusion—available at most magic dealers—is a pouch with a hidden pocket. Place anything flat or flexible in bag and the item magically '*changes*' into a different item.

Any time learners are required to make a list, ask them to write the tasks that must be completed on sticky notes. Collect those notes. Place them in the bag. Then produce a pre-prepared list of completed items from the hidden change bag pocket.

For financial training, learners can list items to be budgeted on cards. Place the cards in the change bag. Then produce the '*dollar bills*' that will be saved through effective budgeting.

Make It Magical

learnertainment® Tip 39:

Use magic to illustrate key points or recapture attention.

The *Needle Thru Balloon* illusion consists of a super sharp, thin needle that easily penetrates any balloon without popping it.

Use the *Needle Thru Balloon* to foster creativity. Ask the learners if they believe that you can push the needle through the balloon. Whether they reply, *"Yes,"* or *"No,"* demonstrate that it can be done. Then explain, *"The only limits are what we place on ourselves."*

This illusion is also ideal for situations when you need to recapture attention. The act of piercing a balloon without breaking it is so captivating that the learners can't help but return their attention to you.

Learnertainment® Tip 40:

Use magic to conclude the learning.

The *Magic Coloring Book* is a reasonably priced illusion in which coloring book pages change from blank, to black and white, to full color.

Use it to illustrate how much the attendees have learned by saying, *"When we began today, your knowledge was a blank slate* (show blank pages). *As we went through the day your knowledge grew* (show black and white pages). *And now look at how much you have learned* (show colored pages)."

My book *Show Biz Training* provides more information and templates for adding magic to learning.

The Learnertainment® Pocket Tip Book

Principle: *The Environment Talks*

Action Step: *Stage The Surroundings*

The Environment Talks

Learnertainment® Tip 41:

Make the learning environment an irresistible invitation to learn.

Learners are often uncomfortable entering the learning environment. Learning requires admitting knowledge gaps, in front of strangers, in an unfamiliar and cold room, to facilitators that may control their future.

Many people also have negative memories of school. They may even worry about their own ability to learn. When you consider all these factors, it's amazing that learning can occur at all.

Light up your classroom with color, props, music, and pleasant aromas. Make it instantly inviting to all who enter and you will disarm learner apprehension.

Stage The Surroundings

Learnertainment® Tip 42:

Do a walk through of the environment prior to the event.

See the learning environment as your learners will see it. Walk the hall they will walk. Place your hands on the door they will open. See what the room looks like when they open the door. Look at the walls, the floor and the trainer platform. Sit in the seats. Check the lighting and temperature levels. Verify that the learners will be able to see you, each other, and the projection system.

When you find issues, correct them. Every moment your learners are distracted by comfort issues is a lost learning opportunity.

My book *Show Biz Training* provides more information and templates for successfully staging learning.

Lenn@OffbeatTraining.com

The Environment Talks

learnertainment® Tip 43:

Control every element in the learning environment.

Every element in the learning environment either supports or undercuts the learning. Trash on the floor, sticky table surfaces, junk in the corner, barren walls, and tangled computer cables all deliver a perception of sloppy instruction. Learners will occasionally lose focus and look away from the learning. When they do, ensure that what they see supports your message.

Clean the room. Pick up the junk. Hide the cables. Place content related posters on the walls. Bring the room to life with color and music. The result will be more focused learning.

Stage The Surroundings

learnertainment® Tip 44:

Know the support staff and honor their contributions.

Make friends with the administrative personnel, the food servers, the audio-visual technicians, and the custodians. If support staff is assisting in the learning environment, get to know them. Thank them for their contribution.

Recognize and honor the hard work these team members do to make you look good. They will gladly assist you if and when you need their help.

Lenn@OffbeatTraining.com

The Environment Talks

Learnertainment® Tip 45:

Use every teachable moment.

The non-instructional moments in a learning program are opportunities to communicate your message. Thirty minutes prior to the official start time, play themed music. Fifteen minutes prior, begin a slide show or video. During breaks, run a slide show of quotes of wuzzles related to your learning topic. At the end of your presentation, play themed music to '*dance*' your learners out of the room.

The non-instructional moments in a learning program are opportunities to communicate your message. Use them.

The Learnertainment® Pocket Tip Book

Principle: Sound Trumps Sight

Action Step: Mix In Music

learnertainment® Tip 46:

Use music to increase learning results.

Music may be the original language. It certainly reaches us at a deep, personal, emotional level. Where words communicate thoughts, pitch and tone communicate emotion. Music is present in almost everything we do. It is also often missing from the learning environment. Music—when used properly in learning environments—establishes and maintains positive moods that increase learning results.

Read Tips 47-58—drawn from my book *Training With a Beat*—to discover musical applications that make learning more effective.

Mix In Music

learnertainment® Tip 47:

Use music to establish a positive learning environment.

As stated in Tip 40, the learning environment can be an uncomfortable place. The sooner you can disarm learner apprehension, the sooner effective learning can begin. Music fosters positive emotions that disarm these anti-learning defenses.

Learners who walk into your classroom and immediately feel comfortable because of the music you play, will be ready to listen.

Sound Trumps Sight

Learnertainment® Tip 48:

Use music to minimize negativity.

Learners react negatively to some subjects. Most of us have experienced situations where learners are forced to attend, are suspicious about our motives, or feel the program is a waste of their time.

Music reaches past intellectual blocking mechanisms and engages your learners. Up-tempo rock is ideal for eliminating this negativity.

Mix In Music

Learnertainment® Tip 49:

Use music to foster creativity.

Music is ideal companion for brainstorming. It helps learners relax, focuses their creative abilities, and provides soundscapes to attach memories to.

Use positive sounding, mid-tempo, reflective new age, light jazz, or Baroque music to encourage creative thinking.

New Age works from artists like George Winston or Keiko Matsui, jazz from Fourplay or Spyro Gyra, and Baroque music from the *Bach for Breakfast* or *Mozart for Morning Coffee* albums all fill this need.

Learnertainment® Tip 50:

Use music as a metaphor for the subject being taught.

Metaphors are created when one item is compared to another so that the concept of the first item becomes more understandable.

Adults have accumulated a depth of experience that serves as a framework for learning. Metaphors tap into that knowledge base. Music—through the lyrics of an appropriately selected song—provides a holistic, memorable image of the subject being taught.

Mix In Music

learnertainment® Tip 51:

Use music to practice repeated tasks.

From boat rowing, to fruit picking, to assembly line work, to jogging, people throughout the world synchronize music with repetitive movements.

Any activity with a timed sequence can be set to music. Once consistency has been established, accelerate the musical tempo. This will help your learners gain speed and grow their skills.

Sound Trumps Sight

Learnertainment® Tip 52:

Use music to enhance game show activities.

Music makes game show activities seem less test-like and more enjoyable. Use music to cue the steps that take place during games. Play music as players come to platform, spin a game wheel, roll dice, and return to their seats.

Music sets parameters when you ask questions and require answers within specific time limits. It also hypes the awarding of prizes. Fanfare music effectively communicates that the game has ended.

Audio sound effects are also effective. *'Dings,' 'Ahhs,' 'Ohhs,'* swells, chimes, and applause all add value and excitement to the experience.

Mix In Music

learnertainment® Tip 53:

Use music to manipulate moods.

Music can change the dynamic of your learning environment. It encourages learners to move about, relax, calm down, or become motivated.

Use fast rock music to creates better moods and stimulate energy after focused, tiring learning segments. Use slow, minor key music to bring learner energy levels down after exciting, aggressive activity segments.

learnertainment® Tip 54:

Use music to block ambient noise.

Background noise can distract learners from the task at hand. Quiet music during solo reflection and small group discussions absorbs some of the conversational rumble.

Music places an audio wall between groups, creating a sense of privacy for small group discussions, making conversations more satisfying, and encouraging participants to say what they feel.

Mix In Music

learnertainment® Tip 55:

Use music to aid memorization.

When tied together, words and music engage a large portion of your learners' brainpower. The brain regions required to process sound, words, meaning, emotion, and rhythm must all become engaged to comprehend the music.

Most children learn their alphabet by singing the letters. Adults have forgotten this effective tool. Tie your key points to a song and your participants may retain your message.

Music is also an effective study aid. By recalling the music played while studying, learners may also recall the material.

Sound Trumps Sight

Learnertainment® Tip 56:

Use music to enhance reviews.

Slow Baroque or early Classical music, pulsing at a rate parallel to that of the human heart—around 60 to 80 beats per minute—helps decrease brain activity while creating a relaxed state of awareness. This relaxed state is ideal for reviews.

Musical reviews are effective prior to quizzes, during reviews, as a refresher, and during that supposedly sleepy time after lunch when the body is tired but the mind is alert.

Mix In Music

Learnertainment® Tip 57:

Use music to celebrate the completion of learning.

The completion of any session or module is a cause for celebration. The learners have achieved a milestone. They should have the opportunity to celebrate their success.

Music is an ideal companion for these moments. It effectively concludes the segment while making the completion more notable and celebratory.

learnertainment® Tip 58:

Use music with lyrics appropriately.

Lyrics draw attention. Use songs with lyrics only when you want your learners to focus on the music.

Use songs without lyrics when you want the music to fade into the background.

Songs with lyrics are ideal for metaphors, breaks, and sing-a-longs. Songs with lyrics should not be used when you want learners to talk to each other or engage in solo reflection.

My book *Training With a Beat* provides more information and templates for the application of music in learning.

The Learnertainment® Pocket Tip Book

Principle: Laughter Produces Positivity

Action Step: Harness Humor

Laughter Produces Positivity

Learnertainment® Tip 59:

Use laughter to engage your learners.

Even if you ignore humor, your learners will find it, sometimes at your expense. The need to laugh in a classroom is so strong that learners will laugh at even not-so-funny jokes. They do this to release tension.

Laughter has a number of benefits. It allows learners to discuss negative emotions in a humorous, enjoyable, and non-threatening manner. It builds relationships. It brings you and your learners together with common insights. It keeps your learners focused because they miss the joke if they don't pay attention. Finally, it engages both holistic and logical brain cells. A joke is a twist of logic that must be both visualized and translated into language.

Harness Humor

learnertainment® Tip 60:

Learn and apply the joke teller's sequence.

All humor shares a defined sequence: introduction; supporting information; unexpected conclusion; listener surprise; laughter.

A joke begins with an introductory statement that introduces the subject. Next comes supporting detail that leads the listener down one path of assumptions. Those assumptions are upended in the unexpected conclusion. Here the listener realizes that the previous information has a dual meaning. That realization causes surprise. The surprise releases as an involuntary response called laughter.

Tip 61 suggests ways to study humor. Tips 62-75 provide templates for applying the joke teller's sequence.

Laughter Produces Positivity

learnertainment® Tip 61:

Study humor and try it out in your learning programs.

Expose yourself to humor on a regular basis. Use a funny daily calendar, read the comics, collect funny signs and sayings, look for workplace stupidity, listen to the late night comedians, and join a '*joke-of-the-day*' list. You will begin to notice common formulas. It will then become easier to deliver your own funny lines.

The joke telling formulas listed in Tips 62-75 will help you create your own jokes. Try a joke out on your learners. Massage it until it works. Then keep it. Most importantly, have fun. No one expects you to become a professional comedian. Mildly humorous is funny enough.

Harness Humor

Learnertainment® Tip 62:

Add humor by replacing boring words with funny ones.

Some words are funnier than others. Banana is funnier than fruit. Smuckers is funnier than jam. Redenbacher is funnier than popcorn. Turpentine is funnier than paint thinner. Calamity is funnier than mishap. Indubitably is funnier than yes.

Funny sounding words have multiple syllables, hard consonants, and odd cadences. These characteristics make the words humorous.

If given a choice between a funny sounding word and a non-funny word, choose the funny one. It won't create a laugh—they're not that funny—but it will foster a lighter, more comedic, mood.

Lenn@OffbeatTraining.com

Laughter Produces Positivity

learnertainment® Tip 63:

Add humor by inserting a humorous last line into a list.

Lists of procedures, steps, or sequences can be extremely tedious to cover. Break up that monotony by inserting a ridiculous additional step.

If you were listing great composers for example, you could list Bach, Beethoven, and Britney (Spears). The last item in the list comes as a surprise, and, because it is ridiculous when compared to the first two items on the list, causes a laugh.

This technique is also useful during multiple choice quizzes and game show activities. To alleviate tension, place a funny item as the last answer for each multiple-choice question.

Harness Humor

learnertainment® Tip 64:

Add humor by conducting a fake survey.

Learners often expect to be surveyed. A simple comedic formula is to ask your learners, *"How many of you want to know more? Raise your hands. How many of you find this interesting? How many of you wish I'd just shut up and get on with it."*

This formula is also a list of three (see Tip 63 for more information).

Laughter Produces Positivity

Learnertainment® Tip 65:

Add humor by exaggerating the truth.

Humor often results because of an exaggeration or *'twisting'* of an obvious truth. One of the most common exaggerations occurs when the comedians say, *"It was so cold last night that..."*

Any subject can be twisted. If, for instance, your learners complain about the difficulty of a test, you could respond, *"If you think this was bad, you should have seen the last test. It was so tough that even the teacher flunked."*

Harness Humor

Learnertainment® Tip 66:

Add humor by modifying an acronym, slogan, or event name.

Acronyms, slogans, and event names provide good opportunities for humor. You can change a word or two in the acronym to make it funny.

The customer service acronym, *DO IT!* (DETERMINE, ORGANIZE, INITIATE, THANK) could be introduced as DETERMINE, ORGANIZE, INTIMIDATE, THANK. You would then immediately correct yourself and say, *"Sorry ... that wouldn't work!"*

Event names and slogans can also be modified. You could say, *"Today we are 'Learning with the beast,' ... err ... Learning with the BEST! ... Sorry."*

Before you use this formula, verify that your learners will appreciate the joke.

Lenn@OffbeatTraining.com

Laughter Produces Positivity

learnertainment® Tip 67:

Add humor when unexpected problems occur.

An effective way to defuse a technology problem is to thank the competition. If you are, for instance, training Federal Express employees and your computer crashes, you can say, *"I'd like to thank FedEx for providing this opportunity, all of you for attending, and UPS for the antiquated technology."*

Alternatively, if a crash sound comes from the next room and you are instructing UPS employees, you can say, *"Oh, don't worry. That is just FedEx trying to sort their packages."*

Harness Humor

Learnertainment® Tip 68:

Add humor when a learner says something inappropriate.

Off color, insulting, sexual, political, and other inappropriate comments take the air out of a room. In response, learners will often gasp, laugh nervously, or freeze up while they wait to see how you will respond.

If a learner says something inappropriate, respond by saying, *"Shh, this is a family show,"* or, *"For more info call (insert the offenders name) at 555-1212."*

Any of these simple responses will alleviate tension, deliver a mild rebuke to the offender, and refocus your learners on the material.

Laughter Produces Positivity

learnertainment® Tip 69:

Add humor when trying to sell product or collect money.

If your lesson includes an opportunity for the learners to contribute money, purchase products, or order services, you can lighten the '*sales pitch*' aspect of the conversation by making up a fake charity.

For instance, if you have children you can say, *"Anything you contribute will go to a good cause: the SMSC fund ... that's Send My Son to College ... and boy do I need to get him out of the basement."*

This small joke will alleviate the tension learners may feel about a sales pitch.

Harness Humor

learnertainment® Tip 70:

Add humor by repeating famous TV commercial lines.

The television commercials your learners are familiar are a ready source of comedic material. Depending on the situation, *"Don't worry. You're in good hands with me" or "I've never done this before, but I did stay at a Holiday Inn last night."* The humor comes from the unexpected connection you make between the commercial and your subject matter.

Before you use this formula, verify that the commercial you intend to spoof is locally known.

Laughter Produces Positivity

learnertainment® Tip 71:

Add humor by showcasing your shortcomings.

Learners sometimes place the instructor on a pedestal. This adulation can become a barrier. A common technique for building rapport is to highlight your own shortcomings.

If you wear a loud shirt or tie, ask, *"Can you hear me over my tie?"* If you are short, say, *"I'll keep it short"* If you are bald, say, *"I hope my forehead isn't blinding you. Can you see me?"*

Be careful, however, not to overdue it. Too many of these comments may suggest that you lack confidence in yourself. Also, avoid these comments if one of your learners also shares the characteristic you are making fun of.

Harness Humor

learnertainment® Tip 72:

Add humor by cautioning your learners.

Learning programs sometimes require you or a learner to try something that may seem dangerous, difficult, or ridiculous. The uniqueness of the situation may make your learners feel tense.

To break the tension, step away from your focus on the task and offer a fake caution. Warn, *"Don't try this at home. Your family will disown you," "Don't try this at home. Leave the stupidity at work," "Don't try this at home. Your neighbors might call the police,"* or any other suitable caution that your learners will appreciate.

Laughter Produces Positivity

learnertainment® Tip 73:

Add humor by sharing a quote.

Quotes are wonderful humor devices that do the funny lifting for you. Humorists like Benjamin Franklin, Mark Twain, and George Carlin make you seem funny without you having to tell a joke.

And, when a funny quote is the last in a series of quotes (see Tip 63), it provides a comic perspective different from what more serious experts have said.

Harness Humor

learnertainment® Tip 74:

Add humor by showcasing a cartoon.

Cartoons are effective metaphors. They illuminate content in a holistic manner that adds value to any learning point.

Cartoons are, however, sometimes so thought provoking that learners forget to laugh. If your learners focus on the point the cartoon is making, and engage in deep thought as a result, don't worry about the size of the laugh. The cartoon has done its job.

When you find a cartoon directly related to your material, use it. Verify, however, that you have legal permission before you display it or place it into a slide show presentation. Resources like my own *Cartoons for Trainers* book & CR-ROM combo provides royalty free cartoons for legal use in learning.

Lenn@OffbeatTraining.com

Laughter Produces Positivity

learnertainment® Tip 75:

Avoid common humor traps that offend learners.

Humor is easy to deliver if you follow a few simple cautions. Never announce that you are going to tell a joke. Because laughter results from surprise, announcing the joke guarantees it will not be funny. Humor should also be situation-based or self-directed. Never make fun of your learners, your colleagues, your bosses, or your organization. Avoid political, religious, or ethnic jokes. Even if some of learners laugh, other will be offended. Because people laugh at risqué lines out of discomfort, they are not appropriate in the learning environment.

Finally, be yourself. Allow your naturalness to create the humor for you. My book *Show Biz Training* provides more joke creation templates that will improve your performance.

The Learnertainment® Pocket Tip Book

Principle: Professionalism Produces Results

Action Step: Perfect Your Performance

Learnertainment® Tip 76:

Use the *PREPARE*™ formula to uncover and solve problems.

Presentation disaster can happen to anyone. In entertainment, there is an old saying that *'the show must go on.'* To make the show happen regardless of any problems that occur, entertainment professionals follow a formula. It can be summed up in the acronym *PREPARE*™ (*PLAN, REHEARSE, EXPLORE, PROTECT, ACCEPT, REACT and ENJOY*).

Use this sequence to prepare for and confront any presentation challenges you face. Tips 77-83 explain the formula.

Perfect Your Performance

learnertainment® Tip 77:

Prevent presentation disaster by *PLANNING* your presentation.

The Plan is the most critical part of any performance. Stage productions go through months of development before rehearsals begin. Movies are storyboarded before filming starts. Football coaches work out the plays before training camp opens.

Presentations, although not as involved, still require planning. The best planning tool is a script. Outlines are functional, but lack specificity. Any production contains detail not apparent in an outline. A script helps you experience the instructional flow, identify the materials you need, and uncover potential problems. When you have a workable script, you are ready to move on to the next *PREPARE*™ step.

Lenn@OffbeatTraining.com

Learnertainment® Tip 78:

Prevent presentation disaster by *REHEARSING* your presentation.

Entertainment professionals perform so effortlessly because they rehearse so much. They examine the script line by line to plot the logistics of the performance. They determine where the props should be placed. They identify how each item and person will get from point '*A*' to point '*B.*' Finally, they spot and connect loose ends in the script.

Learning professionals do not have to practice as much. You should, however, practice more than you do. Although run-throughs are tedious and time consuming, they are time well spent. Rehearsals find and solve problems before disaster strikes. Once you have begun rehearsing, you can begin to focus on to the next *PREPARE*™ step.

Perfect Your Performance

Learnertainment® Tip 79:

Prevent presentation disaster by *EXPLORING* problems that might occur.

Even if you've worked through—and rehearsed—your script, something always goes wrong. Entertainment professionals work through potential showstoppers in advance. They try to identify all the issues that could prevent them from delivering a flawless performance.

Take additional time to list out any potential problems you may experience. The more problems you can identify, the less opportunity you will leave for unwelcome surprises. When you have identified the potential showstoppers, you are ready to move on to the next *PREPARE*™ step.

learnertainment® Tip 78:

Prevent presentation disaster by *PROTECTING* yourself against potential problems.

Show biz professionals know that the broadcast, live performance, or concert must go on. To ensure this happens, they devise multiple back up plans. You should too.

Once you have identified a potential problem, you can protect yourself from it by devising an alternative. But that solution may also develop a problem. Protect yourself again by devising a solution for the solution. Ask yourself, *"What's the backup plan?"* Then ask yourself, *"What's the backup plan for the backup plan?"* Finally ask yourself, *"What's the backup plan for the backup backup plan?"* When you know those answers, you are ready to move on to the next *PREPARE*™ step.

Perfect Your Performance

learnertainment® Tip 81:

Prevent presentation disaster by *ACCEPTING* any problems that occur.

In Actors Improv, the unexpected is welcomed as a gift that leads to new discoveries. It is an axiom among magicians that the magician has upper hand because the audience doesn't know what is supposed to happen. The audience will think the unexpected was planned. This fact gives the performer a decided advantage.

Accept whatever happens as a gift and you will maintain your composure. You can then calmly move on to the next *PREPARE*™ step.

Lenn@OffbeatTraining.com

Professionalism Produces Results

Learnertainment® Tip 82:

Prevent presentation disaster by *REACTING* to solve the problem.

When the unexpected happens, take charge. React with the confidence that comes from knowing you are prepared.

The amount of preparation you have engaged in will make it easier to quickly solve the problem. Your learners will be impressed by the amount of preparation you put into your presentation. The problem, and your reaction to it, will make you look more professional. When you have reacted calmly, you are ready to move on to the next *PREPARE*™ step.

Perfect Your Performance

Learnertainment® Tip 83:

Prevent presentation disaster by *Enjoying* the situation.

If you have, as listed in Tips 77-82, *Planned*, *Rehearsed*, *Explored*, *Protected*, *Accepted*, and *Reacted*, the final step is to Enjoy whatever happens.

You control the dynamic so relax and place your focus where it belongs, on your audience. Your good grace and class under pressure and admired. Your evaluations may in fact be the best you have ever received.

Lenn@OffbeatTraining.com

learnertainment® Tip 84:

Don't waste time on history.

For many learners, what happened ten, five, or even a year ago, is ancient history. The only valid reason to share our stories, workplace traumas, and insider observations is because that information makes a must-be-learned point. The learners are not very interested in why something used to be done differently.

When you share outdated information, your learners may absorb and apply the wrong information. Focus on the specific immediate criteria required for learner success. Stay in the present.

Perfect Your Performance

Learnertainment® Tip 85:

Instead of telling your learners, get them to tell you.

Learners rarely leave a program saying, *"I wish that guy had talked some more."* When you say it, you own it. When they say it, they own it.

Start with what your learners already know about the subject. Present them with problems and challenges that build on their prior experiences. Ask them to figure out what the answers are. If someone doesn't come up with the correct solution, ask others what their solution would be. Validate the learners for the information they provide. Then, fill in the blanks.

When you make your learners figure it out, you work less as they learn more.

Learnertainment® Tip 86:

Every piece of information you deliver must be critical for learner success.

We're subject matter experts. We know too much. It makes it hard for us to see what is relevant to a novice. It is tempting to include interesting background information. But when you learn to drive a car, you don't need to know how to change the spark plugs. The fine details—even if they are fascinating—can wait until the learner is able to drive the '*vehicle*.'

Before you share a piece of information, ask yourself if that information is absolutely critical for learner success. If not, leave it out.

Perfect Your Performance

Learnertainment® Tip 87:

Stay focused on the learning topic.

Learners resent it when we don't get to the point. When we meander, the information becomes hard to follow. Our learners don't know—having never been exposed to the content before—what information is important and what is not. They try, as a result, to absorb everything and get lost.

What your learners most need from you is a tight focus on the concept with the details clearly aligned. Then they can concentrate on the '*must-haves*' instead of the '*might-haves*.'

Professionalism Produces Results

learnertainment® Tip 88:

Give your learners time to practice.

We've all been in situations where more content needs to be delivered than time allowed. When this happens, learner practice is often discarded. Instructors keep talking in a forlorn attempt to give the learners every morsel of knowledge.

You may be driven—knowing that this is your only chance to reach this audience—to give your learners the full benefit of your expertise. But talked is not learned. Your learners need to try it. Give them that time.

learnertainment® Tip 89:

Deliver relevant applications.

Information that does not provide immediate, relevant, and identifiable application is wasted. Most learners have such a difficult time absorbing information that anything but immediate application becomes background noise. When they cannot tell how something relates to their needs, they stop listening.

Verify that there are applications to everything you teach. And then, help your learners identify those applications.

Professionalism Produces Results

Learnertainment® Tip 90:

Use the *PERFORM*™ formula for reconnecting with your audience and your purpose.

Delivering any training program, class, or speech over and over again can become a facilitation bore. It is, however, the first delivery for your audience.

Your learners deserve your best performance. But how do you insure that each and every delivery is as fresh as the first?

The acronym *PERFORM*™ (PLAY, EXPLORE, REFINE, FOCUS, OWN, RECONNECT and MOVE) is a formula for getting yourself aligned with, and excited about, the material you teach. Tips 91-97 explain the formula.

Perfect Your Performance

learnertainment® Tip 91:

Reinvigorate your delivery by *Playing* for the audience.

In the entertainment industry, Performers who have tired of their role tune the mechanics of the role out and the audience in. By focusing on the audience, the performer becomes one with the audience's experience.

During learning, the material—not the instructor—is the show. Do not overshadow your learning points. Those points—and the success of the connections those points make with the learners—determine the success of a learning event. Focus on the reaction of the audience to your material and you will experience the excitement of learning through their eyes.

Lenn@OffbeatTraining.com

Professionalism Produces Results

learnertainment® Tip 92:

Reinvigorate your delivery by *EXPLORING* the alternatives.

Performers are always exploring alternatives. Actors, who are told when to enter, how to stand, where to look, what to say, and which emotion to portray, keep their performance fresh through subtle variations in the inflection, movement, or look.

Fortunately, we don't have a director telling us what to do every step of the way. If you become bored with your material, embrace this freedom and deliver the material in different ways. Stand in a different spot. Use a different vocal inflection. Add humor. Run an activity with a different twist. If an actor can stave off boredom, you can too.

Perfect Your Performance

learnertainment® Tip 93:

Reinvigorate your delivery by *REFINING* your technique.

Comedians rarely settle for what worked the night before. Once a joke works, they search for a second joke to add. Once that joke works, they search for a third, and then a fourth. The process of refinement never stops. This constant improvement keeps their act fresh.

A robotic delivery telegraphs a lack of enthusiasm for the material. Your skills are not set in stone. Continually refine your delivery. Look for a better place to stand, a more flowing hand gesture, a more relevant grouping of words, and a clearer way to conduct the discussion. This continued search for refinement can help you conquer boredom.

Lenn@OffbeatTraining.com

Professionalism Produces Results

learnertainment® Tip 94:

Reinvigorate your delivery by *FOCUSING* on emotion.

Classical musicians play the same notes, exactly, flawlessly, in performance after performance. Instead of focusing on the mechanics of the notes, the classical musician focuses on the emotion within the notes.

You may present the same material so often that your mouth repeats the content without conscious awareness (much as your car finds its way to work). It's your brain's procedural memory at work, and it's a source of liberation. Once the procedural memory takes over, you can concentrate on the emotional message behind the words. Then you will be able to deliver your message with genuine passion.

Perfect Your Performance

learnertainment® Tip 95:

Reinvigorate your delivery by *OWNING* the material.

You can spot a bored actor. He goes through the motions required by the script but clearly doesn't own the words he speaks. The critics call it *'walking the part.'* In contrast, great actors tunnel inside the character so deeply that the actor disappears.

Learning professionals—regurgitating pre-ordained talking points—also become bored. Learners can tell if you are *'walking the part.'*

You have an obligation to tunnel into the material, to believe it, and deliver it in a spontaneous, fresh, and original manner each and every time.

Professionalism Produces Results

learnertainment® Tip 96:

Reinvigorate your delivery by *RECONNECTING* with your purpose.

Performers work for the art, not the pay. It's a calling, not a job. Learning professionals also work for a variety of higher purposes (i.e. helping people, sharing information, and continued self-development).

The reason you became a trainer, teacher, or speaker can be obscured over time. If you no longer enjoy the work, if you are bored by it, try to reconnect with your original purpose. That purpose is your guide to an enthusiastic delivery.

Perfect Your Performance

learnertainment® Tip 97:

Reinvigorate yourself by *MAKING* a move.

Most of the world views a job as a multi-year situation. Performers think in terms of *'gigs'* that come and go. Professional artists fear something worse than unemployment: losing their creative edge. Performers who lose interest in the performance quit.

Likewise, learning professionals who are bored should make a move. Try training a different subject. Learn a new skill. Change careers. If you have tried *PLAYING*, *EXPLORING*, *REFINING*, *FOCUSING*, *OWNING*, and *RECONNECTING* and none of it has worked, make a move. You owe it to yourself and your learners.

My book *Show Biz Training* provides more information and templates that will improve your performance.

Lenn@OffbeatTraining.com

Learnertainment® Tip 98:

When critics accuse you of using gimmicks, agree.

Critics are the bane of every show biz professional, except when they give a good review. Learning professionals also want good reviews. When you use Learnertainment®, your approach may be criticized as gimmicky.

If you are confronted with the *'gimmick'* criticism, reply, *"Exactly. What's your point?"* The critic will likely be speechless. Then add an explanation, *"Of course it's gimmick. But so is advertising. And television. And movies. Everyone has a gimmick. That's how I capture, maintain attention, and it will deliver superior results."*

Perfect Your Performance

learnertainment® Tip 99:

When critics accuse you having too much fun, tell them that fun makes the message stick.

Explain to the critic that fun makes learning palatable. It is the medium, not the message. Content is king. Fun will, however, help people relax. It makes their learning more enjoyable, meaningful, and memorable.

Entertainments with little content are like cotton candy: tasty when eaten but quickly forgotten. Great entertainments have more staying power because they transform and invigorate. Learning should be that way too. Use it to make your message stick.

Professionalism Produces Results

Learnertainment® Tip 100:

When critics warn that their people just want the facts, show them they are wrong.

This criticism often comes from previous bad learning experiences. Everyone wants to have a good time. They do not, however, want their time wasted with mindless fluff.

Introduce Learnertainment® slowly. Allow the critic—and your learners—time to grow comfortable with the techniques. Have a legitimate reason for every fun element you use. If it isn't relevant, leave it out. Above all else, get the learners involved and engaged in their own learning experience.

Eventually, the critic won't be able to imagine the experience without the fun.

Perfect Your Performance

learnertainment® Tip 101:

Appreciate your opportunity to make a difference.

Stop being so serious. Relax. Enjoy life. It's too short anyway. You woke up today! It's already a good day.

Savor the rare opportunity you have to help people learn and grow. This is a noble profession. Be proud to be a part of it.

It is true that soldiers, police, firefighters, and doctors do more for people's critical needs. They safe lives.

You also meet a critical need.

You save lives from being wasted.

That's noble too.

Lenn@OffbeatTraining.com

The Learnertainment® Pocket Tip Book

Finale: *Two Questions*

Credits: *Additional Resources*

Finale

Two Questions:

Is your learning so enjoyable that you could charge admission?

Would you give a ticket to your training to someone you liked and admired?

If you answered *"No"* to either of these questions, how do you think your learners feel? ... And, what are you going to do about it?

In Medieval times people believed that when mischievous sprites heard you wish for something, they would make the opposite happen. People would—just in case the sprites were listening—wish each other bad luck. Entertainers are notoriously suspicious. They still do it.

Assuming you are going to become a Learnertain™ your audience, and in keeping with show biz tradition, I have one closing wish for you.

Break a leg!

Lenn@OffbeatTraining.com

Additional Resources

Want more? Lenn can help:
- Dynamic presentation skills training
- Up close and personal one-on-one eCoaching
- Creativity and brainstorming experiences
- Insightful instructional design consulting
- Effective team competency workshops

Visit www.OffbeatTraining.com or email Lenn@OffbeatTraining.com

www.OffbeatTraining.com learning resources:
- *ASTD InfoLine: Music as a Training Tool* book
- *Cartoons for Trainers* book & CD-ROM
- *Game Show Themes for Trainers* music CD
- *Show Biz Training* book
- *TrainerSounds*™ Desktop Music Dashboard
- *Training With a Beat* book
- *The CLOUT Competencies Inventory*©

Other training materials vendors:
- Creative Presentation Resources learning tools, www.presentationresources.net.
- Tool Thyme for Trainers learning tools, www.tool-trainers.com.
- Hank Lee's Magic Factory magic supplies, www.magicfact.com.
- Smile Templates PowerPoint® templates, www.smiletemplates.com.
- Teacher Pay Teachers lesson plans, www.TeachersPayTeachers.com